Olympic Dreams
Atlanta '96

A Chronicle in Poetic Form of the Centennial Olympic Games

by

Gary Stewart Chorré

Do your best!

Mary S. Cherra

OLYMPIC DREAMS: ATLANTA '96
Copyright © 2008 Gary Stewart Chorré
Layout by Adam Rubinstein

ISBN-10: 1-934415-92-8
ISBN-13: 978-1-934415-92-4

Printed in the United States by Morris Publishing®
3212 East Highway 30
Kearney, NE 68847
1-800-650-7888

Contents

1   *Jim Thorpe: Greatest Athlete in the World*

2   *The Mind*

3   *The Trials*
    Mary Slaney has returned...

4   *With four Olympics to his credit...*
    A bright red apple...

5   *Behold a superman...*
    Without so much as a back-flip...
    The decathlon has Dan O'Brian...

6   *In the women's 100m, Gwen Torrence...*
    At the 100m hurdles, Gail Devers...
    And of course golden girl Joyner-Kersee...
    Coach Vanderveer will steer...

7   *There are many more...*
    The Olympic Torch

8   *Atalanta: The Huntress*

10 *Ali*
    Lighting the Torch

11 *Watching the Big Show*
    Fond Remembrance

12 *First American Gold Swimming,*
    Men's 400m Individual Medley
13 *Cycling, Women's Road Race*
14 *Gymnastics, Women's Team Compulsories, USA*
    At these Olympic games…
15 *Swimming, Women's 100m Breaststroke*
16 *To do your best…*
    Rowing, Men's Single Skulls Repecharge, Preliminaries
    Gymnastics, Men's Team, Compulsories
17 *At the committee of Olympic Glitches…*
18 *Basketball, Men's Team*
    Weightlifting, 64kg
19 *Swimming, Women's 100m Backstroke*
    The scalpers pace; tickets held high…
20 *Swimming, Men's 4 x 100m Relay*
21 *Soccer, Women's Team*
    Greco-Roman Wrestling, USA Assistant Coach Bob
        Anderson and his Girlfriend, Judy Mundy,
        Get Married
22 *Greco-Roman Wrestling, 130kg*
    Tennis, Women's Preliminaries
    Roaming the streets…
23 *Gymnastics, Women's Team Events*
27 *Soccer, Men's Team*
28 *Swimming, Men's 100m Butterfly*
    Swimming, Women's 200m Individual Medley

29 *Pins, pins and more pins.*

30 *Gymnastics, Men's Individual Events*

31 *Swimming, Women's 4 x 100m Medley Relay*
    Equestrians, Three Day Team Event

32 *Two million people with an invitation…*

33 *Swimming, Men's 200m Individual*
    Swimming, Women's 200m Backstroke

34 *Basketball, Men's Team, USA*

35 *Swimming, Women's 4 x 200m Freestyle Relay*

36 *Grab your tickets and a Coke…*
    Gymnastics, Women's Individual All-Around

38 *Baseball*
    Platform Diving, Women's 10m,
    Preliminaries

39 *Shot Put, Men's Final*
    Humid heat, oppressive on head and feet.

40 *Race Walking, 20k*
    Swimming, Women's 50m Freestyle

41 *Swimming, Men's 200m Backstroke*
    Swimming, Women's 200m Butterfly

42 *Friday night and all is right…*

44 *The Bomb*

46 *Judy Hinson: Tribute to a Living Angel*

47 *The Decision*

48 *Diving, Women's 10m Platform*

49 *Track and Field, Women's 100m Finals*

50   *Track and Field, Men's 100m*
       Track and Field, Women's Heptathlon
       A human sea engulfing me…

51   *Marathon, Women's*
       Track and Field, Men's High Jump

52   *Water Polo*
       Gymnastics, Men's Floor Exercise

53   *Gymnastics, Men's Pommel Horse*
       Cycling, Men's Sprint

54   *Late at night, with no energy left to deplete…*
       Gaffari, America's ambassador of goodwill…

55   *Gymnastics, Men's Rings*
       A Tribute to Women's Gymnastics

56   *Gymnastics, Women's Balance Beam*
       Gymnastics, Women's Floor Exercise

57   *Diving, Men's 3m Springboard*
       The crowd's aroused…
       Track and Field, Men's 400m

58   *Track and Field, Men's Long Jump*

59   *Centennial Park Reopens: Tuesday, July 30, 1996*

60   *Weightlifting, Over 108kg, Super Heavyweights*

62   *Track and Field, Women's 100m Hurdles*
       Wrestling, Freestyle, 57kg

63   *The hot spark of an Olympic fire…*
       Basketball, Women's

64   *Boxing, Flyweight*
       Wrestling, Freestyle, 100kg

65   *Track and Field, Men's 200m, Preliminaries*
       Track and Field, Men's 800m

66 *Hezekiel Sepeng becomes…*
        The streets are full, with nary a car in sight…
67 *Cycling, Men's Road Race*
        Track and Field, Men's Discus
68 *Football, Men's Semifinal*
69 *At Centennial Park*
        Track and Field, Women's 200m
70 *Buzzing crowd surrounds…*
        Track and Field, Men's 200m
71 *Field Hockey, Women's Finals*
72 *Football, Women's Finals*
        Atlanta, Southern gem…
73 *Track and Field, Men's 400m Hurdles*
        Wrestling, 130kg, Preliminaries
        Track and Field, Decathlon
75 *Ray Charles sings so sweet…*
        Track and Field, Steeplechase
        Synchronized Swimming
76 *A Poet on the Box*
77 *Baseball*
78 *Wrestling, 130kg*
        Tennis, Women's
79 *You've got an invitation to party…*
        Handball, Men's Team
81 *So tired, still wired, can't sleep…*
82 *Centennial Park Concert, Friday Night*
        Indoor Volleyball, Women's
83 *Tennis, Men's*
        Track and Field, Women's High Jump

84 *Track and Field, Men's Javelin*
Cycling, Men's Individual Time Trial
Track and Field, Women's 1500m Relay

85 *Centennial Park: Agricultural Exhibit*
Lights sparkle off the smiling faces…

86 *Basketball, Men's Team*

87 *Muhammad Ali Receives*
an Honorary Gold Medal

88 *Centennial Park Concert: Little Feat*
Basketball, Women's Team

89 *Football, Men's Team*
Rhythmic Gymnastics
Purple blossoms in the rain…

90 *Boxing, 71kg*
Track and Field, Men's Marathon

91 *Sitting in a corner of my mind…*
Closing Ceremonies

92 *Pack it up, it's time to go…*
It's sad to see the Games end…

95 *Final Words*

Once you step out there, unless you're dying, you finish the dance.

Mary Joe Fernandez, USA
Tennis Player

Jim Thorpe: Greatest Athlete in the World

On lucky May 28, 1888,
this day, a giant was born.
His visage, the world's Halls of Fame, would eventually adorn.
Delivered as a twin,
his brother's untimely death forced him to grow up as one.
A strapping youth having fun
running barefoot in the Oklahoma sun.
In 1904, Carlisle Institute, to higher education, opened the
     door.
Finally discovered,
coach "Pop" Warner offered him the opportunity to become
     so much more.
They began training for the Olympic Games
and a chance, upon the world stage, for exposure and fame.
With the U.S. Team, in 1912,
upon the *Finland* they sailed.
Once in the spotlight, Jim Thorpe did excel.
With a superhuman effort, in the city of Stockholm,
the other athletes he did dethrone.
The only double-trouble man
to win the pentathlon and decathlon.
King Gustav V said it all
when he made the call:
"You, sir, are the greatest athlete in the world."

The Mind

It's the mind, not the shape;
that is where you'll find your fate.
Ever wonder why some are great and other small,
many hesitate and never hear the call?
Even the lucky few
who are born to a penthouse view
find that their place in society
depends on what they do with this temporary opportunity.
Some say history makes the man.
There are times when this is true
though I have seen a few, within our midst,
who would reach the highest branches of any tree,
scale the top of hill or mountain peak
and hardly speak of, or even notice, the extent of their feat.
Matters not if you are in the lead or far behind,
I say to you, it's in the mind.
This does not mean your path will be clearly marked,
a stroll in the park on a bright sunny day.
Regardless of what you start out with in life,
'tis not easy for pauper or king to fight through the strife.
The opportunity to sink or swim is always there.
The question is, will you dare?

The Trials

The trials bring out heartache and smiles,
courage, compassion and wiles.
From the sidelines we safely watch
as the egos rise and fall.
Each has heard the trumpet's call,
pushed body and mind to the wall.
The tape is stretched;
the mark quickly drawn.
For some this summer will bring sweet slumber.
Others retire in tears
to rest weary head
upon lonely bed.

Mary Slaney has returned and is knocking on the door.
She collided with barefoot Zola Budd back in '84.
'88 saw her last Olympic race.
A world record runner who has never gotten hold
of an Olympic gold.
In '92 she sat on the sidelines, oh, so blue.
Now in '96 she's determined to beat the Olympic jinx.
Last chance for her day in the sun.
Maybe this time she'll be the one.

With four Olympics to his credit
Carl Lewis has been around so long
some think he's getting a wee bit old
to sing this song.
In the finals of the 100m he gets a cramp.
Tough luck, champ.
The long jump is his time to dance.
For three straight Olympics he's snatched the gold.
This could be his last chance.
In anticipation the crowd stills.
Sand flies,
as upon the long jump pit are fastened all eyes.
They take the mark.
Carl Lewis still has the spark.
By an inch he's in.
With a chance to sink
he chose to swim.
The first American man in track to partake in five.
The crowd's abuzz, an excited hive.

A bright red apple for Albuquerque's Olga Apell.
At 10,000m she finishes second to Kathrine Fonshell.

Heading to Atlanta,
for these two girls, all is well.

Behold a superman with shoes of gold.
At 400m, Michael Johnson has won a consecutive fifty three
and in the 200m he intends not to be controlled.
This is a man the whole world wants to see.

Without so much as a back-flip
two gymnasts, the trials, have skipped.
National champions both,
the injured pair have been given a bye.
Shannon Miller and Dominique Moceanu,
to the American consciousness, are new.
The Olympic girls haven't hit the big scores
since way back in '84.
Maybe this time there'll be some magic on the floor.

The decathlon has Dan O'Brian soaring on.
In the pole vault,

the event that broke him in '92,
over the bar he flew.
As the best all-around athlete in the world,
he hopes to be hailed
when in Atlanta the flags are unfurled.

In the women's 100m, Gwen Torrence
puts in a blistering performance.

At the 100m hurdles, Gail Devers
never wavers.

And of course golden girl Joyner-Kersee,
in Atlanta, we will again see.

Coach Vanderveer will steer
as a new Dream Team

makes the scene.
Lobo's no hobo.
And with the likes of Leslie and Swoopes,
America's women will dominate in hoops.

There are many more.
All with great scores.
In the gymnasiums and on the fields
it appears the rest of the world
will have to yield.

On To Atlanta!

The Olympic Torch

The torch is a healing source.
The crucible of life
where all our burning desires
may be cleansed, consumed then scattered
to the swirling winds of fate.
Harmless ash and smoke
drifting weightless toward eternal heavens

as it lays a blanket of hope
across the red clay fields of a modern Olympus,
firmly rooted in the ancient landscape.
The torch's journey is a hands-on pilgrimage of the people,
bonding us together as one
on its 15,000 mile parade,
stopping in city and town,
passing through village and hamlet,
where the unbroken thread of civilization
connects a modern people through the ancient ritual of sport,
cleansing the collective soul of a world gone mad.
Seventeen days where the community of mankind
may gather and be glad.
One people striding hand in hand
with brother and sister from many walks and all lands.

Atalanta: The Huntress

Atalanta, fleet of foot.
Wondrous maiden, so fair,
with flowing locks of golden hair.
All men do yearn,
one and all, for their turn.
A chance at the dance of eternal love.
Though none, as yet, has landed a dart

upon the mark next to loving heart;
her grace and glory to capture for his own.
Pray to the spirits beyond the sky
or shed woeful tears from lonely eye.
Matters not, the extent of your desire.
Atalanta, uncontrollable as the sun's fire.
Though there may be one
with spirit bright enough to stare into a blazing sun.
A way for the turtle to snare the hare.
Victory relying not upon mere speed
but the seed
of a plan hatched by one
with thoughtful mind nimble as a reed.
Golden apples, three,
Aphrodite did provide thee.
Mystical means to tempt one so fair.
Atalanta, beautiful huntress, maiden without a care.
In the race for her heart
our brave lad did let go,
dropping golden fruit,
one by one, before her feet so fleet.
Tempted thus, she would stop and stoop,
snatching from the ground golden apples, oh, so rare.
In this way he beat, to the mark, his golden hare.
the victory line, first to cross,
that he might win the dare.

Atalanta the huntress,
beautiful maiden, oh, so fair
that day became a wife.
To live and love through the glory and strife
beneath the glimmering rays of a golden sun.
Two joined together as one

Ali

Sting like a butterfly,
float like a bee,
then you can rhyme like Ali and me.
He was the greatest.
No doubt in my mind.
If you can't see that,
you gotta be blind.

Lighting the Torch

The Games soon to begin,
the torch is lit.
In gleaming sun,
athletes stand oiled and fit.
Anticipation crackles through thick muggy air.

An electric spark piercing the din.
Trumpets sing, let the Games begin.

Watching the Big Show

Sitting in the cheap seats.
Perspiring from the close heat.
Responding anxiously to the throbbing crowd.
Straining to hear.
Noise so loud, am unable to comprehend
as jumbled words go unheard.
Another round of applause,
then a pause.
Straining craning, in a rubbernecked attempt to see
through and beyond the human trees.
Still, no one can say I did stray,
missing out on the big play.
Ticket stubs, in sweaty palm, remain
to stake eternal claim.

Fond Remembrance

Oh, how I'll gush
upon reflected glory of the feat.

Pushed and shoved in the rush,
a crowd so large
tens of thousands were left out in the street.
But I was there,
perched upon the edge of a wooden chair,
basking in its glorious sheen.
The greatest show that's ever been seen.

First American Gold Medal Swimming, Men's 400m Individual Medley
(Tom Dolan, USA, Gold)

Tom Dolan,
a man with a plan.
A quick dip in the pond
and he did respond.
The asthma-man is first in the door
as, for his country, he does score
a shiny medal of gold
for all to behold.
In this steamy Southern summer
may there be another and another...

Cycling, Women's Road Race

(Jeannie Longo, France, Gold)

Go, go, Longo!
For a medal, to France
she gives a chance.
With pounding heart and legs
she surges ahead,
pushing the pack far back.
6 miles to go.
Go, go, Longo!
Still in sight, still in mind.
At this stage she can't afford the urge
to be kind.
All of a sudden,
with a superhuman surge,
Longo is gone.
Bye bye, so long.
On this day of cycling
the Sultan did win.
A sweet bottle of French wine
crosses, first, the finish line.

Gymnastics, Women's Team Compulsories, USA

Karolyi may not be holy
but in gymnastic circles his shadow hits every wall.
Under his guidance our tiny women stand tall.
Dominique, so petite.
Ah, but this girl can compete.
From the past,
a huge shadow the greats do cast,
but this young lady's star
shines light near and far.
And Miller, what a thriller.
Grace without haste.
Supple limbs,
her routine sings.

At these Olympic games,
even though you don't get to compete,
you've got the best seat.
One that beats the heat.
In this great country of ours
we all get to watch Atlanta's Olympic show
on color T.V's with remote control.
In office, factory and store

we speak of the economy no more.
For seventeen days, we roll up our sleeves,
and vicariously participate,
staying up late
to catch a glimpse of the best in the world
as they run, jump and hurl.

Swimming, Women's 100m Breaststroke
(Penny Heyns, South Africa, World Record and Gold)

Penny Heyns reigns.
A golden swan,
across the clear, wet, blue does skim
as mere mortals attempt to swim.
And shed narry a tear for Amanda Beard,
teen princess revered.
With loving smile she gave her all
and though her medal be made of silver
I'll be so bold
as to uphold
that before she gets too old
to her bosom, she'll clutch the gold.

To do your best, have got to be a little more than smart.
It takes heart.
Better not waste energy in a public pout,
'cause body and mind must be one throughout.
All who compete have the desire to win,
yet second place on the victory stand is no sin.

Rowing, Men's Single Skulls Repecharge, Preliminaries

Row, row, row your boat.
Skim that water, float float, float.

Gymnastics, Men's Team, Compulsories

Bagiu,
Albuquerque loves you.
On the high-bar
you are a star.
And with chiseled physique, Umphrey
scores points for his country.

No disdain
for Blaine.
True Blue,
he came through.

❈

At the committee of Olympic Glitches
someone forgot to throw the switches.
The buses run right on time
but not to where you need to go.
They take you somewhere else for your dime
or so late they get you there
that you just don't care.
If you yearn for an update on the score
forget the computer screen,
accurate information, from it you shall not glean.
And without a dozen forms of I.D.
the days events you shall not see.
Can this be the same Olympic committee
that daily shines
and sticks in our minds
with flashy ads upon TV?

Basketball, Men's Team
(USA defeats Angola, 87-54)

Dream Team is right!
Sleep-walking through the game tonight.
All that talent and they still need to push and shove
to dominate sparrows and doves.
Been reading too many of their own press releases.
Looks as if they are afraid to wrinkle,
in their bitches, the creases.

Weightlifting, 64kg
(Naim Suleymanoglu, Turkey, World Record and Gold)

This Hercules has a rocket in his pocket.
Don't be a jerk and besmirch
his diminutive size,
for this man is a giant when he strives.
His world record is clean
as he reaches out to snatch the gold.
All of Turkey is enthralled.
The "Pocket Hercules" will be remembered regardless of his Naim.

Swimming, Women's 100m Backstroke

(Beth Botsford, USA, Gold)

Beth, you are the best.
With a smile, to boot!
You're neat.
Beaming family so proud.
You stand head-and-shoulders above the crowd.
Fifteen years old and you've won the gold.

The scalpers pace; tickets held high,
tickling the sky.
Small crowds surround
asking venue and price
as, from the economic pie,
American entrepreneurs take a wee slice.

Swimming, Men's 4 x 100m Relay

*(Jon Olsen, Josh Davis, Bradley Schumacher,
Gary Hall, USA, Gold)*

400m 'tween destiny and here.
A tradition of thirty years
on the line.
Success and failure a thread so fine.
Determination upon stoic faces
as our team prepares for the races.
Four men standing at the ready
as tension fills moist air.
Hometown crowd, oh, so loud.
With all this pressure can they remain steady?
Olsen is the first to dive and strive,
struggle and kick, through the foam.
Davis is next to grace the pool.
Oh, man, this race is cool!
Schumacher is no slacker.
A hard working man who can.
Hall goes sailing through the sky,
surging ahead,
to the roar of the crowd does he fly.
Records fall
as he hits the wall.
They faced the challenge and met the call.

Soccer, Women's Team

(USA vs. Sweden, 2-1)

In football,
America's girls came to play, one and all.
Oh, so quick
when they dribble, pass and stick.
Shot on goal.
USA is on a roll!
Our soccer team
is supreme.
Another vanquished power
heads for the shower.
Let the world beware,
in soccer our women are there
and we care.

Greco-Roman Wrestling, USA Assistant Coach Bob Anderson and his Girlfriend, Judy Mundy, Get Married

Anderson got married to Mundy on Tuesday.
Wrestling to the mat their doubt,
in a winning round, loneliness goes down for the count.
With this match, eternal bliss can't miss.

Greco-Roman Wrestling, 130kg

(Alexander Karelin, Russia, Gold, vs.
Matt Ghaffari, USA, Silver, 1-0, Overtime)

Siberian bear without hair.
Mess with him I would not dare.
Body and eyes of cold steel.
A red bear, with the will to kill,
drags the gold back to his lair.

Tennis, Women's Preliminaries

Monica Seles says she's back.
Recovered from the horror
of a madman plunging a knife into her back.
At these games she's way ahead of the pack.

Roaming the streets with a pair of sore feet.
At night it gets a wee bit cold
and my stomach, for several hours, has been on hold.
Hungry for a meal that won't deplete
my shrinking stash of silver and gold.

Turn a corner and there it is,
a landmark that hits the spot.
In Atlanta, The Varsity is the place to go.
Hamburgers and fries, juicy and hot.
They even have big-screen TVs to watch the show.

Gymnastics, Women's Team Events

The nymphs of old did dance and sing.
Today they've come to the gym
determined to win.
America's best put to the test.
Young girls all grace and smiles.
They've trained for years
coming many a mile.
Win or lose they are the essence of style.
Marching in line,
standing tall,
with anxious anticipation
the hometown crowd cheers them all.
Jaycie stands silently alone,
then it begins.
Working the uneven bars, the ice is broken, the crowd sings.
Kerri takes a turn and she does shine.
Karoli thinks she's divine.

Dominique, such a tiny speck,
she takes wing
and upon the bars does swing.
Man, this is great, what a show.
American girls, way to go!
Amy Chow, oh, wow!
Somersaults twisting high,
she touches the sky.
Shannon Miller is a winner.
Her routine's a killer.
This night is a glorious dream.
The throng yells and screams.
Dominique Dawes draws nothing but awes.
On the balance beam these girls are supreme.
One by one, they nail their routines.
Still the Russians will not fold.
This is bigger than that cold war of old.
The crowd hovers on the edge of their seats.
All eyes are glued to the monitors
in anticipation of every score.
Next event the teams take to the floor.
Phelps and Amanda get points galore.
Dominique and Dominique,
oh, can these girls compete.
Once again Miller delivers,
though she almost takes a fall.

The air is taut with tension.
Will we lose our momentum
or will the girls be bold
and the precious lead hold?
Pandemonium reigns.
The crowd goes wild.
They're standing in the aisles.
Next, the girls are vaulting.
A quick sprint to the horse
then up and away they fly.
Somersaults through thin air;
a feat most would never dare.
The Russians are still there,
knocking on Glory's door.
Awesome, Dawes gets more applause.
Then wee Dominique gets a chance, unique,
to post the numbers high upon the scoreboard
that will capture for America a golden horde.
She stumbles; the crowd sighs.
Another chance.
Again she loses her balance
and falls.
A collective moan rises from the country's living rooms,
bars and halls.
Kerri's turn.
Now we will learn.

Karoli extols.
The crowd,
its collective breath, does hold.
Flying through the ether,
time slows.
A country's pride,
upon her outstretched wings, does ride.
With a sickening thud she hits the mats and falls.
She's hurt.
It's bad, real bad.
The crowd stands.
The entire country stalls.
A hush.
Eternal seconds.
Karoli needs to know,
can she go.
Strug shrugs and nods yes.
One more chance at the big dance.
A quick sprint
and in a flash
there she goes,
up and over,
folks, it's clover.
Landing on one foot
she does the deed,
then falls.

In agony she crawls.
A warrior goes down
and a legend rises from the dust.
Upon her shield an American hero is carried away.
Through the pain, joy and tears
the country cheers.
A magnificent seven
carrying the torch into the new millennium.
Amanda Borden,
Shannon Miller,
Kerri Strug,
Dominique Dawes,
Amy Chow,
Jaycie Phelps,
And Dominique Moceanu,
America pays tribute to you.

Soccer, Men's Team
(USA vs. Portugal, 1-1, USA Eliminated)

Men's football,
tough call.
They came to play.
Gave it their all.
On the fence, all tied up,

no chance for the cup.
Singing a sad song,
they're gone.

Swimming, Men's 100m Butterfly
(Denis Pankratov, Russia, Gold)

A nuclear explosion ripping through
the cool, clear blue.
The "Russian Rocket" blasts past mere mortals,
roaring straight through history's portals.
No one had a ticket to pass Pankratov.
It's useless to get cross.
All did their best.
No one really lost.

Swimming, Women's 200m Individual Medley *(Michelle Smith, Ireland, Gold)*

Michelle, pray tell,
a double rainbow you wear so well.
She traveled across the great blue sea
and now she's going for number three.

The swimmers explode
and the crowd does, too.
Lungs and muscles pushed to the hilt
as they boogie full-tilt.
When they hit the wall,
Michelle is the one.
A well-earned day in the sun.
The emerald green was once serene
but now, oh, wow,
in all the pubs, what a scene!
Ireland finally has a dream queen.
Michelle Smith, you're cool,
and a real tiger in the pool.

Pins, pins and more pins.
Buying and trading Olympic pins
may not be a sin,
but it's awfully close to a pinddiction.
Two million spectators and 50 million pins,
enough to create plenty of grins.
So many styles you can't get them all.
Better be careful or to pindemonium your wallet will fall.

Gymnastics, Men's Individual Events

Vitaly Scherbo is back.
Courage this man does not lack.
One month he lost,
as his wife, death's border, she almost did cross.
True love, such a cost.
Whatever happens in the medal rounds,
one thought resounds:
this man is a winner
with priorities firmly planted in the ground.
Nemov, to a good start, is off.
Greatness with grace
but he can't keep the pace.
These are all worthy men.
In the end,
there is but one
and Li Xiaoshuang has won.
On the high-bar he was a star.
Pumping clenched fists in the air,
his victory to declare.

Swimming, Women's 4 x 100m Medley Relay

(Beth Botsford, Amanda Beard, Angel Martino,
Amy VanDyken, USA, Gold)

On Beth's labored breath we start the flow.
And Amanda ain't no panda.
"Teddy" Beard struggles with all her might.
On Angels' wings, Martino swings.
The fans in "Amy's Army" row stroke for stroke with "General"
    VanDyken.
The world record doesn't quite fall
as she hits the wall.
Still, it's another golden day
for the U.S. of A..

Equestrians, Three Day Team Event

(Wendy Schaeffer, Sunburst; Phillip Dutton, True
Blue Girdwood; Andrew Hoy, Darien Powers;
Gillian Rolton, Peppermint Grove; Australia, Gold)

Equestrians, elegance and grace without haste.
The greatest athletes in the world prance and dance upon all
    fours
as the Australians capture the high scores.
Sleek and strong, they clear the rails

to the crowd's cheers and hails.
Though there is one fact that's a bit of a shame:
not a sneaker contract to their name.
A rubdown and a little extra hay,
their only claim for a victorious display.
All day the Aussies rise to a worthy ride.
At these Olympics they hit their stride.
Down Under,
they'll surely feel the roaring thunder.
On to Sydney!

Two million people with an invitation to party.
Even the cops are cool.
They've got the patience of saints escorting a crusading army.
A friendly but authoritative voice their number one tool.
On the streets of Atlanta you see every variety
of uniform and badge in front of thee.
But of the constables' protection the rest of Georgia must be
    barren.
In village and hamlet the good folk are surely despairin'.

Swimming, Men's 200m Individual Medley
(Attila Czene, Hungary, Gold)

As Chelsea, Hillary and "The Big Guy"
watch from the stands with attentive eye,
the swimmers take their mark.
False start.
Again, they reline,
on the edge, ready to shine.
Up and back they track.
Fierce competitors who cut no slack.
At the breast,
Yani is the best.
On the run,
Atilla is the one.
In the end Czene
has that winning sheen
as a ravenous Hungary
feasts upon the glean.

Swimming, Women's 200m Backstroke
(Krisztina Egerszegi, Hungary, Gold)

Egerszegi is ready.
Power stroking,

the boiler stoking.
A whirling windmill
makes the others appear still.
Once again the little mouse
builds a golden house.
This Hungarian queen
reigns supreme.

Basketball, Men's Team, USA

Charles Barkley throws a shoe to the crowd.
Better than throwing a fit.
A kid grabs it,
oh, so proud.
Once there was a woman
who could have turned it into a house.
Her entire family,
within its confines,
would fit snug, cozy as a mouse.

Swimming, Women's 4 x 200m Freestyle Relay

(Trina Jackson, Chistina Teuscher, Sheila Taormina,
Jenny Thompson, USA, Gold)

Jenny Thompson leads the team out to the pool.
The stands are full.
Our women are pumped,
ready, the rest of the world, to thump.
Jackson takes the mark,
hoping to open destiny's door
in lucky lane four.
The Germans grab the early lead.
Christina comes on strong,
pushing America ahead at the halfway mark.
What a spark.
The spirit of the team is supreme.
Sheila puts on a display.
It's Germany and the USA
Thompson hits the water with a solid lead.
What a stroke.
She ain't no slow-poke.
Heading for home,
the crowd's attention doesn't roam.
The president smiles
as the throng goes wild.
Chalk up another gold
for America's women so bold.

Grab your tickets and a Coke.
These are all friendly folk.
In any language it's all the same.
These are the whole world's Olympic Games.

Gymnastics, Women's Individual All-Around
(Lilia Podkopayeva, Ukraine, Gold)

Dominique, so petite,
with a smile quite sweet,
but don't let it fool you;
determination made of steel,
a combination with appeal.
Shannon Miller gave it her best
until the floor did her in.
With teary eyes,
her chance dies.
Dominique Dawes has few flaws
in her graceful routine
'til she stumbles on the floor,
in the lead no more.
Kochetkova works so hard.
It's her time to shine.

This night she is alight,
lost in the shadow of the Americans no more.

As number two, Kochetkova hits the floor
knocking on the first place door.
On the vault she does fault
and drops back down
with a frown.

Mo Huilan is China's number one.
Now she leads the world.
With honor and pride she reaches full stride.
The floor routine is her last.
She must do her best
to wrest the gold from all the rest.
A slip and step out of bounds.
Her personal anguish resounds.

Podkopayeva has worked so long for this chance.
Nobody expected Cinderella to get the last dance.
A final dash with elegance and class.
All of Ukraine, as queen, she will reign.
On top of the world,
she is the best.
Olympic champion.
Number one.

Baseball
(USA vs. Japan, 15-5)

For the USA the number Seven
was a slice of heaven.
They cut loose
and tightened the noose,
cooking their opponents' goose.
Hitting seven home runs in the muggy Southern sun
makes America's pastime a whole lot of fun.

Platform Diving, Women's 10m, Preliminaries

Becky Ruehl is cool.
No fear in this Kentucky princess
as she dives into the crystal pool.
Twirling, swirling, curling.
No sweat,
these girls are all wet.
Such grace in motion,
America will never forget.

Shot Put, Men's Final

(Randy Barnes, USA, Gold)

Barnes, the competition, disarms.
With a shot heard round the world,
into the record books he puts the measure of his arm.

Humid heat, oppressive on head and feet.
Commercialism so pervasive and crass.
Public transportation, forget it, just pass.
Lines long enough to make a saint faint.
Yet these frustrations are inconsequential and small
when you consider the trail of courage
tread by athletes, short and tall.
A lifetime of work for a momentary chance to exert,
to prove themselves against the best.
The lucky few will stand,
embracing upon the victory stand,
adding a bit of glory
to their country's story.

Race Walking, 20k
(Jefferson Perez, Ecuador, Gold)

Walking, not talking.
Looks a little tipsy with those swinging hips.
Still, they walk faster than I can sprint.
Determined struggle for position in the sun's glint.
Mr. Perez,
raw courage, displays.
Now the man from Ecuador
is obscure no more.
A gold medal and fame
for his country to claim.

Swimming, Women's 50m Freestyle
(Amy VanDyken, USA, Gold)

Amy VanDyken marches out to the pool.
A serious woman, determined and cool.
Martino is there,
an angel with a cheshire smile,
hoping to win in style.
This is a race with a very fast pace.
Wam, bam, VanDyken slams.
A record-setting win by the length of a hand.

Swimming, Men's 200m Backstroke
(Brad Bridgewater, USA, Gold)

Sliding by, upon their backs,
it's a good thing they're not wearing cowboy hats.
Arms churning, lungs burning.
At the wire,
the rest of the world does retire.
A knockout punch for the USA
as Brad makes us glad today.

Swimming, Women's 200m Butterfly
(Susan O'Neil, Australia, Gold)

Michelle Smith arrived a little late
Oh, well, this race is a matter of fate.
On the mark, they're ready.
O'Neil is for real.
Steady Susan is a'crusin'.
Four years of work,
for one race, to exert.
No one can touch her pace,
A golden monarch with wings of steel
matched with a fiery will.
Australia's sassy lassy

this day is happy.
On to Sydney!

Friday night and all is right.
Everywhere the crowds are friendly and loud.
A woman with a sprained ankle sits on the grass without
    complaint.
Even the drunks behave with restraint.
Kids frolic in the open fountain.
All the wise men have come down from the mountain.
Everywhere you go,
it's as if, each person, you know.
What a shame there has to be an end to this show.

The Bomb

We interrupt this program for a special news bulletin from our National News Desk. Dateline, Atlanta: terrorists have struck at the heart of the Olympic Games. At approximately 1:20 AM EST, a terrorist bomb exploded at Centennial Olympic Park in downtown Atlanta, Georgia. Reports of casualties are sketchy at this time, but at least one death has been confirmed and estimates of serious injuries number as high as several hundred. Pandemonium is rampant throughout the Olympic Center Complex and it may be several hours before accurate casualty figures are available. Atlanta area hospitals are urgently requesting that all E.R. and Trauma Unit doctors and nurses report to their stations immediately. All units of the Fulton County Sheriff's Dept., Atlanta Police Dept., Georgia Bureau of Investigation, Georgia National Guard, US Marshalls, US Border Patrol, A.T.F., and the FBI have been placed on Red Alert. All athletes have been ordered to return to the Olympic Village Complex. Authorities warn travelers of possible delays on flights out of Atlanta International Airport as well as the train and bus stations. The president has been awakened and briefed. He has expressed his deepest regrets over the injuries and loss of life and requests that everyone remain calm. I repeat: terrorists have struck at the heart of the Olympic Games. A bomb exploded in Centennial Park at approximate 1:20 AM

EST. Casualty figures are sketchy at this time, but at least one death has been confirmed. Please stay tuned to this station for further bulletins. We now return you to your regularly schedule program.

Judy Hinson: Tribute to a Living Angel

Judy was there that fateful day
when a crazed man did splay
our innocence into a thousand shrapnel fragments.
With these cowardly monsters our patience is spent.
The bomb killed one
and Judy was there.
A time to despair
and run
from an exploding sun.
Thousands crowded for the exits.
Men did push and shoulder
to reach the escape outlets,
safe from the sight and sound of bloody terror.
The bomb blast assaulted Judy's eardrums
and for a moment she was numb.
A woman fell in front of Judy, hard, to the ground.
There were screams of horror all 'round.
As the wounded woman hit the red earth
a bouquet of flowers and camera landed beside her.
In a situation that few incur
destiny offered Judy a clear choice.

For her life, to run,
or stay the course, be brave,
cold fear to shun,

another's life to save.
Off-duty nurse, Judy Hinson went right to work,
mindful only of another's hurt.
With the help of an off-duty doctor
they checked for a pulse.
there was none.
No breath was left.
Unable to save the slain one (Alice Hawthorne, 44, deceased)
Judy placed a blanket over the crimson-stained dress,
then the lady's lifeless legs did she cross,
so as to offer a sense of dignity
in the face of this tragic insanity.
Judy then turned toward the spot
where bouquet and and camera had set
and they were gone.
To this day, no one knows where.
Does anyone care?

The Decision

A decision had to be made.
Disband the Games
or go on with the Olympics.
There was no easy answer.
To continue might place more lives at risk.

Stopping the Olympic Games now would be giving in to the
    terror.
The Olympic movement would for all intents and purposes be
    finished.
There would never be another Olympiad that would run its
    full course.
The sick and evil among us would strike every four years
to disrupt the world stage and gain attention.
The decision was made.
I believe it to be the right decision.
The Games must go on!

Diving, Women's 10m Platform
(Fu Mingxia, China, Gold)

Clark has the spark.
Radiant blue eyes
cannot disguise
the heart of a lion
with the grace of a lark.
Barely making the final 16,
she never gave up,
continuing the dream.

Mary Ellen is honored,
a medal to have earned,
unlike some crybabies who whine
if upon bronze they dine.
A nurturing father's struggle with cancer
helped create a focused performer
with her values in line.
Mary Ellen, America thinks you are divine.

And Annika Walker
doesn't faulter
as she snatches German-Silver.

But it's Fu Mingxia who carries the day,
springing to snatch the gold.
Back to Back Olympic perfection so bold.

Track and Field, Women's 100m Finals
(Gail Devers, USA, Gold)

Gail Devers wavers not
in this summer sun so hot
as she shakes off a blistering performance
by Gwen Torrance.

Track and Field, Men's 100m
(Donovan Bailey, Canada, World Record, Gold)

Donovan Bailey
does rally,
the world record to best.
He glides head and shoulders above the rest.
From his shadow none could escape.
The world's fastest man is first rate.
Way to go, Dono.

Track and Field, Women's Heptathlon

Jackie Joyner-Kersee pulled a hamstring today.
She wanted to go on
but her husband/coach said no way.
Today she sings a sad song.

A human sea engulfing me.
Living and giving the way it's supposed to be.
Left and right,
black and white,

poor and rich,
mingle and pass without a hitch.
For seventeen days the world displays
a unity we call community.

Marathon, Women's
(Fatuma Roba, Ethiopia, Gold)

Another miracle for Fatuma.
With the day's results, Roba is delighted.
Her golden necklace has all of Ethiopia excited.

Track and Field, Men's High Jump
(Charles Austin, USA, Gold)

Today, Sotomayor
wasn't there as a contender.
The eight-foot man
a bad ankle did slam.
And Partyka has a broken heartica.
Austin is awesome.
The top spot he does assume,
flying high above the full moon.

Water Polo

(Spain vs. Croatia, 7-5)

Spain, it's plain;
when put to the test,
you lay the others to rest.
In the water polo pool
you are oh, so cool.

Gymnastics, Men's Floor Exercise

(Ioannis Melissanidis, Greece, Gold)

Tonight, a golden victory for Greece
as one man, the competition, does fleece.
Upon the floor Melissanidis
did not miss.
High upon Mt. Olympus,
Ioannis is surely blessed.

Gymnastics, Men's Pommel Horse
(Donghua Li, Switzerland, Gold)

Riding a golden horse through the Swiss Alps,
Donghua Li,
to victory, does ski.

Cycling, Men's Sprint
(Jens Fiedler, Germany, Gold)

Fiedler ain't no fiddler.
When he starts to sprint
the others are pushed to the brink
and from victory shrink.

Track and Field, Men's 400m, Preliminaries

For the fans,
Michael Johnson tosses a pair of golden shoes high into the stands.
Sure hope his sneaker company understands.

Late at night, with no energy left to deplete,
yet nobody's ready to sleep.
Sweaty, sticky, wet humanity.
A state of mind beyond insanity.
Pulsing crowds,
moving, growing, flowing.
On the street it's a steady beat.
Two million people without a curfew
party all night until the first shades of morning dew.

"America's silver medalist in weight lifting goes to the hospital
to visit the injured daughter of the woman killed
in the bombing."

Gaffari, America's ambassador of goodwill,
spent the day in the hospital
visiting and comforting terror bomb victims.
He could have been playing, out on a whim,
but his heart is bigger than his head.
Today, compassion and goodwill he does spread.

Gymnastics, Men's Rings

(Yuri Chechi, Italy, Gold)

A long time since the medal of '64.
All of Italy
is counting on Yuri
to crash the treasure vault's door.
Perfection may be impossible in sport,
but this performance earns an A+ on any report.
Such grace on rings,
his guardian angel sings.

A Tribute to Women's Gymnastics

Poor wee girls,
such pain and strain.
A heavy price, giving up childhood
to be this good.
What shall they do for an encore,
when adults they become?
Will we remember them, all and one?
Let's hold them in our hearts and dreams,
when they no longer grace our TV screens,
recalling their courage
and the high price of fame.

Gymnastics, Women's Balance Beam
(Shannon Miller, USA, Gold)

Miller once again delivers.
The country cheers.
A glorious encore to wipe away the tears
before she heads for history's door.
One more time,
Shannon Miller is divine.

Gymnastics, Women's Floor Exercise
(Lilia Podkopayeva, Ukraine, Gold)

Lilia glides
with a smooth graceful stride.
Her composed, classical features cannot hide
the blazing determination deep inside.
All the girls did strive
but Podkopayeva earned her spot
on top
of the awards-stand.
Let's give her a big hand.

Diving, Men's 3m Springboard

(Yu Zhuocheng, China, Silver / Xiong Ni, China, Gold)

Diving and thriving,
as China's double trouble tigers
fight each other for number one,
offering glory to a glowing sun.
X, Y, Z; they do it with ease.
Two silk flags singing in the breeze.

The crowd's aroused.
A sea of t-shirts with faces,
rushing places.
Camera bags and smiles so glad,
such a scene Atlanta has never had.
A friendly riot
without a pilot.

Track and Field, Men's 400m

(Michael Johnson, USA, Gold)

Michael Johnson,
a modern Mercury in golden shoes.

This man has all the right moves.
Cat's eyes with a poker face.
Speed in the lead,
setting a blistering pace.
Boiler stoking,
he ain't joking.
The man cooks.
An Olympic moment for the history books.
Standing up straight
he makes the others, to the party, show up late.
Shiny medal around his neck
is one heck
of a compliment
for his golden accomplishment.
This lion has earned his golden crown.
Let's give him a big round
of applause.

Track and Field, Men's Long Jump
(Carl Lewis, USA, Gold)

In the long jump he's going for four straight;
this man is great.
Physically fit
and mentally lit.

In '84 he was too proud
for America's crowd.
But now, oh, wow!
Maturity in motion,
ready to create some commotion.
After two tries
he's stuck in third place,
a little displaced.
Turning on the charm,
with a mighty leap,
the competition he does disarm.
Olympic medal number nine
is next in line.
Jogging the victory round,
an American flag, broad shoulders, does surround.
In '96 Carl Lewis finally can
be proclaimed America's golden man.

Centennial Park Reopens:
Tuesday, July 30, 1996

A day to return,
listen,
cry and pray.
Standing together in unity

against the shroud of darkness.
In solemn ritual,
a moment of silence does mark
the reopening of Centennial Park
where terror's ugly grasp
the Olympic Games did clasp.
Tentacles of horror and pain,
our faith to drain.
Two dead in the musty dread.
A world at play
now must mourn this day.
These minds of evil shall not prevail.
They must pay.
From the Olympic Games we can't refrain.
Our loss shan't be their gain.
We gather now,
the world as one.
Together we slay the dragon of fear,
holding those injured and lost, to our hearts, dear.

Weightlifting, Over 108kg, Super Heavy-weights *(Andrey Chemerkin, Russia, Gold)*

These men may not be faster than a moving train
but they can lift a locomotive over their heads with hardly a strain.

The only Olympic event where a beer belly is to your gain.
Such awesome strength,
from the ground,
large trees they could wrench.
These supermen earn every pound they hoist.
Straining with furrowed brow so moist.
Such determination on grimacing face,
even gravity is awed by the weight they displace.

Ronny Weller,
what a feller.
Makes the world record fall
and for a moment, as the world's strongest man, he stands tall.
But Chemerkin is a'workin',
bending that bar.
Lifting those rocks, heavy as a car.
This cop is tops,
as he breaks the minutes-old world record.
Once again, the Russian bear
with the iron stare
is the world's strongest man.

Track and Field, Women's 100m Hurdles
(Ludmila Enquist, Sweden, Gold)

Photo-finish at the line.
Devers tried but did not dine.
Bukovec gave it heck,
with Ludimila, running neck and neck.
At the wire, Enquist takes it by a hair,
showing how much she did care.

Wrestling, Freestyle, 57kg
(Kendall Cross, USA, Gold)

Hard-working man,
with a dream in hand,
could not wait for fate.
Wam, bam,
"Gumby" throws his man
and gobbles the gold.
The crowd's enthralled.
Yummy, yummy,
a satisfied tummy.

The hot spark of an Olympic fire
spreads north, south, near and far.
It strikes people walking or driving in a car,
on the bus or the train,
you can feel it even in the rain.
It's in the pitter and excited chatter.
Daily problems no longer matter
when you're soaring,
engines roaring,
on Olympic wings
where a lone angel sings.

Basketball, Women's

(USA vs. Japan, 108-93)

These women are neat.
Solid fundamentals,
they move their feet.
This team plays "D"
then fills the lanes.
Their experience is plain.
They pass the ball.
Whoever is open gets the call.

This is the way the game is supposed to be played.
A great day, especially for Leslie
as she scores a clean 35.
Way to dive and strive.

Boxing, Flyweight
(Floyd Mayweather, USA, defeats Lorenzo Aragon, Cuba)

Mayweather,
light as a feather,
yet tough enough,
with the Cubans, to scuff.
He doesn't know Castro
but he puts on one heck of a show.

Wrestling, Freestyle, 100kg
(Kurt Angle, USA, Gold)

Strained face of sacrifice
shows the struggle
of tragedy, double.
Father and coach must gaze
through heaven's cloudy haze.
This young man deserves our praise.

The match ends, tied one all.
There's an anxious buzz in the hall
as the referee decides the call,
Whose flag will adorn
the victory platform?
Kurt gets the verdict.
The man from Iran
throws a fit
but to no avail, for the judgement does stick.

Track and Field, Men's 200m, Preliminaries

Michael Johnson continues his historic march.
One more day and he goes for the double.
To the other runners this man is trouble.

Track and Field, Men's 800m
(Vebjoern Rodal, Norway, Gold)

Norway's winged surprise
pulls it off right before our eyes.
This Rodal is no red-nosed reindeer.
In cruise control until the stretch,
when, the lead, he did wretch.

With afterburners roaring,
upon open wings soaring,
straight past the other runners he flew.
For Norway it's been many a summer with victories few.
Now Rodal has claimed a shiny medal of gold
to take back to the land of cold.

Hezekiel Sepeng becomes the first black South African to win
a medal in the Olympics as he takes the silver in the Men's 800m.

The streets are full, with nary a car in sight.
It's the same in the middle of the day or late at night.
One huge slowly creeping crowd
and all the stadiums are a wee bit loud.
Every type of Olympic merchandise imaginable
they're hawking at Medieval street corner stands.
What is going to happen to the stuff that doesn't change hands?
September could see the largest garage sale in the land.

Cycling, Men's Road Race

(Pascal Richard, Switzerland, Gold)

Armstrong goes to the head of the pack,
but the three Musketeers aren't far back.
Soon enough they emerge
and, ahead, surge.
Three men in a row;
a triangle of medals to sow.
Legs pump, wheels spin,
a whirling blur of spandex and titanium.
In the final dash,
Sorensen, ahead, does slash,
but he can't lose the other two.
this will be a test of wills
upon two wheels.
Throats, lungs and legs on fire
it's Pascal Richard at the wire.

Track and Field, Men's Discus

(Lars Riedel, Germany, Gold)

The discus we can trace
back to the plains of ancient Greece.
men, big and strong as a modern Hercules

hurl the discus through the breeze.
Spinning faster than a top
they make the wind stop.
With an arm
to charm,
Lars
does impel
the whirling saucer
all the way to Roswell.

Football, Men's Semifinal
(Nigeria vs. Brazil, 4-3, Overtime)

Flavio dives and strives
giving Brazil a thrill.
But Nigeria has the need,
if not the lead.
Africa's best scratches and claws.
With less than a minute, to a tie they draw.
In overtime Nwanko does score
and Nigeria slips through a crack in the door.

At Centennial Park
a party he does hark
as Santana jams
for the fans.
Evil's mark has been stamped out.
10,000 bodies boogie and shout.
The Olympic spirit could not be cowed,
of this fact the world can be proud.

Track and Field, Women's 200m

(Marie-José Pérec, France, Gold)

It would be unfair
not to compare
two such incomparable feats.
Marie-José Pérec is the best.
Duel gold, so bold,
with a fashion statement to boot.
Her double-trouble accomplishment
is in the record books fifteen minutes
before Michael Johnson's race
is ready to start.

In the streets of France,
tonight they dance.
A poor girl who finally got her chance.
This Cinderella
stands as tall as any fella.

Buzzing crowd surrounds.
Anticipation in the air.
Cool mist without a care.

Track and Field, Men's 200m
(Michael Johnson, USA, Gold)

Such a serious man.
But we all know Michael can.
At the mark,
Fredericks is steady in lane 5.
Everyone is ready to strive.
Michael wears a chain of gold around his neck,
so fast, the extra weight, he doesn't fret.
Gun fires and the blocks rock.
Michael stumbles.
The crowd rumbles.

History stammers and gulps.
He recovers; the fire is lit.
A streaking blur
racing around the track faster than Ben Hur.
The other runners are lost in his debris.
One man racing against destiny.
With a world record at the wire,
the crowd he does inspire.
This man is the real deal
with golden appeal.

Field Hockey, Women's Finals
(Australia vs. S. Korea, 3-1)

Hockeyroos and kangaroos,
our hats are off to you.
Through the competition, you sliced
and diced.
Now you're on top,
don't stop.
On to Sydney!

Football, Women's Finals

(USA vs. China, 2–1)

A football free-for-all.
The girls in white
are alright.
Putting on a clinic,
running China to the point of panic.
Capacity crowd
is beyond loud.
The angels must be watching from the clouds.
A stadium filled with tears and cheers.
The flag is raised and hoisted across the field.
With their accomplishment, the girls are obviously thrilled.

Atlanta, Southern gem.
A glowing blossom
hiding amongst hilly pines.
Many voices united under one sign.
A lot of work
for seventeen days to exert.
Plenty of fun,
though rarely do you see the sun.

Track and Field, Men's 400m Hurdles
(Derrick Adkins, USA, Gold)

He may be bald
but his story will be long told.
With resolute face
he poured it on in the final race.
A steely-eyed lunge at the wire.
Determination on fire.

Wrestling, 130kg, Preliminaries
(Andrey Shumilin, Russia, defeats Bruce Baumgartner, USA)

Baumgartner, his heart did break.
Sometimes these things are an act of fate.
He struggled and fought with all his might.
At times it's just not your night.
On the mat, Andrey was alright.

Track and Field, Decathlon
(Dan O'Brian, USA, Gold)

It was in 1912 in Stockholm, Sweden when King Gustav V
declared Jim Thorpe, after winning the Decathlon, the greatest

athlete in the world. Since then only one man may wear the crown of best all-round athlete in the world. The winner of the Decathlon is that man.

Heavy hung the shadow of the pole vault.
The specter of doubt,
Dan O'Brian had to rout.
Clearing that bar
removed some of the old scar.
In the lead,
he still felt the need
to finish strong.
In the javelin he launched a rocket
that flew straight and long.
Still the medal was not yet in his pocket.
The 15,000m run is always the final hurdle.
The longest mile of his life
ended with tears of joy.
A fitting end to the years of strife.
Dan O'Brian had waited so long
to sing this song.
Jim Thorpe's heir: The Greatest Athlete in the World.

Ray Charles sings so sweet.
Doesn't read music off the sheet
but misses nary a beat.
Sweating all the while
with a loving smile.
The crowd roars,
more, more, more!

Track and Field, Steeplechase
(Joseph Keter, Kenya, Gold; Moses Kiptanui, Kenya, Silver)

Kenya sweeps the track
with the rest of the pack,
'cause at home they run, run, run,
in the hot Kenyan sun.

Synchronized Swimming
(USA defeats Canada)

Five minutes of pure perfection.
We will always remember
beauty's splendor.

A pair of twins could not move in such selfsame harmony.
For the eyes a treat much finer than reality.
Transcendent routines
taken to the edge of human extremes.

A Poet on the Box

Hey, hey, what do you say,
a poet gets his Wheaties day.
All the big guys are on the box.
Gee wiz, I think this idea rocks.
I'll even share a space
with someone who can jump, dive or race.
How about me and the girls
with an American flag unfurled?
Or Ali?
That I would do with glee...
...oh, well.
Even in America you should be able to dream.
Fantasize in the extreme.
And if you doubt
my willingness to pout,
am going to hold my breath until they call.
Wait for the phone to ring off the wall,

informing me
there is going to be
a poet on the box.

Baseball

(Cuba vs. Japan, 13-9)

Baseball may be called "America's Pastime"
but I'll bet my dime
it's the Japanese and Cubans
who are groovin'
and to their TV screens a'movin'
for this championship showdown.
Capitalists and Communists struggling for the crown.
With home run fever
the Cubans drop the clever.
Looks like Fidel will party-hearty tonight.
Maybe he'll smoke an illegal cigar
and cruise the streets of Havana
in a 1950s American car.

Wrestling, 130kg

*(Bruce Baumgartner, USA defeats Andrey Shumilin,
Russia; Bronze)*

Yesterday, Shumilin did win.
Today it goes the other way.
An overtime win, so slim.
Though this battle was for bronze
both fought with all their might.
Finally it was Baumgartner's night.

Tennis, Women's

*(Lindsay Davenport, USA, defeats
Arantxa Sanchez, Spain; Gold)*

Davenport is a great sport.
Came to play and do her best.
Wasn't worried about all the rest.
A family so proud
and a cheering hometown crowd.
No matter what,
this piece of history she's got.
She'll fly higher than a golden swan
as an Olympic champion.

You've got an invitation to party.
Dress as you will.
This celebration goes all night
or until you get your fill.
You don't need a ticket,
just step out into the street.
Come downtown and wander around.
Woman, man or child
can boogie and act a little wild.
Everywhere you go
it's a free show.
One thing is clear:
you've got an invitation to party.

Handball, Men's Team
(USA vs. Algeria, 27-26, Double Overtime)

USA all the way!
Can't give up
America is hot.
One more shot.
A score, all tied up, it's overtime.

OVERTIME:
Algeria gets tough.
For America it looks rough,
then the USA SCORES.
Tick, tock, the clock won't stop.
The fans scream and shout.
Tied again, as time runs out.

SECOND OVERTIME:
This is it.
Which team is the most fit.
For America an injured player
hits the floor,
but we're tough; our team won't waver.
Free shot.
Our team is hot.
USA up by one.

Oh, oh, penalty on the old home team.
Red Card;
for the USA this could be hard.
Algeria's big green machine misses a shot.
Our boys they'll beat not.
Fast break, Algeria with the ball, on the run.
They don't get it done.
Up and down the court.

The crowd does exhort.
They're hanging from the rafters.
The noise is unreal.
This is a game with appeal.
All tied up again.
One minute to go! Oh, no!
America blocks a shot.
Ten seconds, counting down.
USA on offense.
3, 2, 1, BUZZ, no time, but wait...
A foul... on Algeria!
America gets a penalty shot.
Now or never, leaping high, fire the bullet, GOAL!!!
USA WINS, the crowd goes wild.
Red, white and blue flags wave.
What a rave.

So tired, still wired, can't sleep.
Run here, rush there,
we've all got to compete
in the spectator Olympics.
Think, talk, listen,
we're all on a mission.
Have to see it all,

don't trip or fall,
take a rest against the wall.
So tired, still wired.

Centennial Park Concert, Friday Night

Louisiana Zydeco, let's go.
Everybody's dancing and prancing,
jumping up and down,
moving all around.
Go, Go, Geno.
Mr. Delafose is Zydeco.

Indoor Volleyball, Women's
(Cuba defeats China, 16-14, 15-12, 17-16; Gold)

The Chinese did fleece
Cuba's Mireya Luis.

Tennis, Men's

(Andre Agassi, USA, defeats Sergi Bruguera,
6-2, 6-3, 6-1; Gold)

Andre has the Olympic spirit.
He aspired
and inspired
us all
with his sharp play and wicked ball.
Not a sloppy point the whole day.
Andre Agassi smashes through victory's door,
winning America's first Men's gold medal since 1924.

Track and Field, Women's High Jump

(Stefka Kostadinova, Bulgaria, Gold)

Kostadinova
goes up and over.
Breaking the record
she is something to behold.
Upon eagle's wings,
snatching for Bulgaria the gold.

Track and Field, Men's Javelin
(Jan Zelezny, Czech Republic, Gold)

Jan is a brave man.
With his spear,
in the rest of us, he instills fear.
He heaves it so far
could hit a bulls-eye on Mars.

Cycling, Men's Individual Time Trial
(Miguel Indurain, Spain, Gold)

Miguel Indurain,
an Olympic medal, can finally claim.
Five times
upon the Tour de France did he dine.
History will remember him as the best of our time.

Track and Field, Women's 1500m Relay
(Rochelle Stevens, Maicel Malone, Kim Graham,
Jearl Miles, USA, Gold)

Individually they've walked a tough mile.
Finally they share a well-deserved collective smile.

With mutual effort the track did glow.
America's girls, way to go!

Centennial Park: Agricultural Exhibit

Cotton was king.
Of its merits the South did sing.
Grows like a weed
then goes to seed.
Leaves of golden brown
with white nectar blossoms.
When cotton was king
the South wore a bejeweled crown
and clasped the hilt of a double-edged sword,
to be used with care.
Now, with the world,
a richly textured history she does share.

Lights sparkle off the smiling faces
as I stop to tie my laces.
Cool evening air,
electricity everywhere.
All is fine
as upon sweet music we dine.

Basketball, Men's Team Finals

(USA vs. Yugoslavia, 95-69)

Dream Team, Dream Team,
finally tested.
That's OK,
they're well rested.
Caddy Shaq,
the boards, is a'crashin'.
Psyched up and angry, Stockton
is a hoppin'.
The refs are a'snoozin'
while Yugoslavia is losin'.
So smooth is "Penny" Hardaway
he appears to be sailing down an open highway.
David Robinson looks cool
in navy blue.
Malone is a bull in a china shop
as upon the other players he does chop.
Reggie Miller hits a big jump shot
yet somehow Yugoslavia is hanging in,
making the US work for everything.
Robinson slams to the crowd's roar
but the lead is a mighty tight four.
Yugoslavia is trying to slip through history's door.
Their chances are slim

'cause the USA owns the court and both rims.
USA,
the fundamentals,
finally does play.
Keep it up and they'll surely win.
"Penny" turns it on
and, in a flash, Yugoslavia is gone,
winning for America another golden stash.

Muhammad Ali Receives an Honorary Gold Medal

At center court, with the world looking on,
Ali gets another one.
A gold medal
made of shiny metal.
The luster will fade
but nothing can tarnish
the glint of his smile
and the depth of his golden heart.

Centennial Park Concert: Little Feat

Atlanta skyline, at dusk, divine.
Little Feat plays music so fine.
Sitting beneath branches that sway to the vibrating beat
beneath a million feet.
Cool breeze,
people at ease.
Simple joys, sublime.
Music, the ear does tease.
Human smiles for miles around.
Listening to that funky Southern sound.

Basketball, Women's Team Finals
(USA vs. Brazil, 111-87)

Our women's team
is the Dream Team!
Svelt and keen,
a well-oiled machine.
The big time show
with plenty of flair.
America truly does care.
Fast breaks and cartwheels,
a Dream Team with appeal.

Football, Men's Team Finals

(Nigera vs. Argentina, 3-2)

All of Nigeria flips
as the green eagle rips
from the rest of the globe
the purple robe
of Olympic champion.
In football,
Nigeria stands above one and all.

Rhythmic Gymnastics

(Ekaterina Serebryanskaya, Ukraine, Gold)

Rhythm stems from the soul.
From these women it does flow.
Gymnasts who enthrall
with banner, rope and ball.

Purple blossoms in the rain.
Buildings high
scrape the sky.
Pine trees.
Two million people at ease.

Boxing, 71kg
(David Reid, USA, KOs Alfredo Duvergel, Cuba)

Reid, a KO did need
as Cuba's Duvergel
was doing rather well.
Throwing a right
with all his might,
David saved America's pride tonight.
Upon the mat, Alfredo glumly sat
as Reid's corner does erupt
in peals of joy.
Ali tells Reid,
"You're a bad boy."

Track and Field, Men's Marathon
(Josia Thugwane, South Africa, Gold)

Nelson Mandela did not run
in the muggy Southern sun.
But Thugwane did
and dedicated the gold
to the man who set his dream free.

Sitting in a corner of my mind,
contemplating,
smack dab in the middle of the largest crowd
the world has ever seen.
Watching the people
as if it were mass in the cathedral.
Living the dream.
Content to sit,
waiting for absolutely nothing to happen.

Closing Ceremonies

Teary eyes,
longing,
a sense of emptiness and great loss.
The stadium is a kaleidoscope of colors waving proud.
The spirit of hospitality continues to pervade.
Michael Johnson carries the US flag
in a marching parade.
Stevie Wonder sings John Lennon's "Imagine."
The ceremony is gorgeous
but I am moist-eyed, drained and sad.
Out of the stadium goes the Olympic flag.

Only one thought consoles.
Sydney is just four years and half a world away.
If I start walking, maybe I'll arrive in time for opening day.

Pack it up, it's time to go.
Some move fast, others slow.
A few may return, others no.
On this final day,
your state of mind reveals what you did sow.

It's sad to see the Games end.
The camaraderie, pain and joy
will live on, in rhyme and song,
long after these frail temples
of sinew and blood are forever gone.
Whatever else may be said, this one fact is true:
At Atlanta, in the summer of 1996, beneath a muggy Southern sun,
for seventeen days, the world did unite as one.

Final Words

"Goodbye, and God-Speed."
William Porter Payne, President,
Atlanta Olympic Organizing Committee

"Well done, Atlanta."
Antonio Samarach, President,
International Olympic Committee

"Thank you Atlanta, for a time divine!"
Gary Stewart Chorré, Poet

Gary Stewart Chorré

American Poet

New Mexico poet and sometimes-actor, Gary Stewart Chorré was born in the state of New York. After attending first grade in London, England, he moved to, and was raised in, New Mexico, where he soon picked up the patterns and behavioral ways of the American Southwest. He was an Albuquerque High School assistant coach in 1984 when that fine institution won the NM Boy's State Basketball Championship.

Gary Chorré calls the world his home, with family, friends and poetry alliances extending from California to Texas; London to Edinburgh; and countless points in between. World travels notwithstanding, he has maintained a strong and enduring base in New Mexico.

Excerpted and edited from an introduction by Ken Gibson,
February 15, 1998